Off The Leash

DIARY2018

Rupert Fawcett

F
FRANCES
LINCOLN

Moon Phases

● New Moon
☽ First Quarter
○ Full Moon
☾ Last Quarter

First published in 2017 by Frances Lincoln, an imprint of The Quarto Group. www.QuartoKnows.com

A catalogue record for this book is available from the British Library

978-0-7112-3883-1

Printed in China

9 8 7 6 5 4 3 2 1

FSC www.fsc.org MIX Paper from responsible sources FSC® C104723

CALENDAR **2018**

JANUARY

M	T	W	T	F	S	S
1	2	3	4	5	6	7
8	9	10	11	12	13	14
15	16	17	18	19	20	21
22	23	24	25	26	27	28
29	30	31				

FEBRUARY

M	T	W	T	F	S	S
			1	2	3	4
5	6	7	8	9	10	11
12	13	14	15	16	17	18
19	20	21	22	23	24	25
26	27	28				

MARCH

M	T	W	T	F	S	S
			1	2	3	4
5	6	7	8	9	10	11
12	13	14	15	16	17	18
19	20	21	22	23	24	25
26	27	28	29	30	31	

APRIL

M	T	W	T	F	S	S
						1
2	3	4	5	6	7	8
9	10	11	12	13	14	15
16	17	18	19	20	21	22
23	24	25	26	27	28	29
30						

MAY

M	T	W	T	F	S	S
	1	2	3	4	5	6
7	8	9	10	11	12	13
14	15	16	17	18	19	20
21	22	23	24	25	26	27
28	29	30	31			

JUNE

M	T	W	T	F	S	S
				1	2	3
4	5	6	7	8	9	10
11	12	13	14	15	16	17
18	19	20	21	22	23	24
25	26	27	28	29	30	

JULY

M	T	W	T	F	S	S
						1
2	3	4	5	6	7	8
9	10	11	12	13	14	15
16	17	18	19	20	21	22
23	24	25	26	27	28	29
30	31					

AUGUST

M	T	W	T	F	S	S
		1	2	3	4	5
6	7	8	9	10	11	12
13	14	15	16	17	18	19
20	21	22	23	24	25	26
27	28	29	30	31		

SEPTEMBER

M	T	W	T	F	S	S
					1	2
3	4	5	6	7	8	9
10	11	12	13	14	15	16
17	18	19	20	21	22	23
24	25	26	27	28	29	30

OCTOBER

M	T	W	T	F	S	S
1	2	3	4	5	6	7
8	9	10	11	12	13	14
15	16	17	18	19	20	21
22	23	24	25	26	27	28
29	30	31				

NOVEMBER

M	T	W	T	F	S	S
			1	2	3	4
5	6	7	8	9	10	11
12	13	14	15	16	17	18
19	20	21	22	23	24	25
26	27	28	29	30		

DECEMBER

M	T	W	T	F	S	S
					1	2
3	4	5	6	7	8	9
10	11	12	13	14	15	16
17	18	19	20	21	22	23
24	25	26	27	28	29	30
31						

CALENDAR **2019**

JANUARY

M	T	W	T	F	S	S
	1	2	3	4	5	6
7	8	9	10	11	12	13
14	15	16	17	18	19	20
21	22	23	24	25	26	27
28	29	30	31			

FEBRUARY

M	T	W	T	F	S	S
				1	2	3
4	5	6	7	8	9	10
11	12	13	14	15	16	17
18	19	20	21	22	23	24
25	26	27	28			

MARCH

M	T	W	T	F	S	S
				1	2	3
4	5	6	7	8	9	10
11	12	13	14	15	16	17
18	19	20	21	22	23	24
25	26	27	28	29	30	31

APRIL

M	T	W	T	F	S	S
1	2	3	4	5	6	7
8	9	10	11	12	13	14
15	16	17	18	19	20	21
22	23	24	25	26	27	28
29	30					

MAY

M	T	W	T	F	S	S
		1	2	3	4	5
6	7	8	9	10	11	12
13	14	15	16	17	18	19
20	21	22	23	24	25	26
27	28	29	30	31		

JUNE

M	T	W	T	F	S	S
					1	2
3	4	5	6	7	8	9
10	11	12	13	14	15	16
17	18	19	20	21	22	23
24	25	26	27	28	29	30

JULY

M	T	W	T	F	S	S
1	2	3	4	5	6	7
8	9	10	11	12	13	14
15	16	17	18	19	20	21
22	23	24	25	26	27	28
29	30	31				

AUGUST

M	T	W	T	F	S	S
			1	2	3	4
5	6	7	8	9	10	11
12	13	14	15	16	17	18
19	20	21	22	23	24	25
26	27	28	29	30	31	

SEPTEMBER

M	T	W	T	F	S	S
						1
2	3	4	5	6	7	8
9	10	11	12	13	14	15
16	17	18	19	20	21	22
23	24	25	26	27	28	29
30						

OCTOBER

M	T	W	T	F	S	S
	1	2	3	4	5	6
7	8	9	10	11	12	13
14	15	16	17	18	19	20
21	22	23	24	25	26	27
28	29	30	31			

NOVEMBER

M	T	W	T	F	S	S
				1	2	3
4	5	6	7	8	9	10
11	12	13	14	15	16	17
18	19	20	21	22	23	24
25	26	27	28	29	30	

DECEMBER

M	T	W	T	F	S	S
						1
2	3	4	5	6	7	8
9	10	11	12	13	14	15
16	17	18	19	20	21	22
23	24	25	26	27	28	29
30	31					

PERSONAL DETAILS

name

home address

telephone

mobile

e-mail

work address

telephone

mobile

e-mail

website

other info

HELLO POPPY
NO, POPPY, THIS ISN'T GOING TO WORK. YOU'RE TOO BIG
NO, I'M NOT
NO, POPPY, PLEASE, YOU'RE TOO BIG
NO, I'M NOT
SEE?
RF

JANUARY • WEEK 1

monday 1	New Year's Day Holiday, UK, Republic of Ireland, USA, Canada, Australia and New Zealand
tuesday 2	Holiday, Scotland and New Zealand ○
wednesday 3	
thursday 4	
friday 5	
saturday 6	Epiphany
sunday 7	

JANUARY

M	T	W	T	F	S	S
1	2	3	4	5	6	7
8	9	10	11	12	13	14
15	16	17	18	19	20	21
22	23	24	25	26	27	28
29	30	31				

monday 8	☾
tuesday 9	
wednesday 10	
thursday 11	
friday 12	
saturday 13	
sunday 14	

HERE HE COMES, GUYS!
SPREAD OUT! SPREAD OUT!
RF

JANUARY • WEEK 3

monday 15	Holiday, USA (Martin Luther King Jnr Day)
tuesday 16	
wednesday 17	●
thursday 18	
friday 19	
saturday 20	
sunday 21	

JANUARY

M	T	W	T	F	S	S
1	2	3	4	5	6	7
8	9	10	11	12	13	14
15	16	17	18	19	20	21
22	23	24	25	26	27	28
29	30	31				

JANUARY • WEEK 4

monday
22

tuesday
23

☽

wednesday
24

thursday
25

Holiday, Australia (Australia Day)

friday
26

saturday
27

sunday
28

GO FOR IT, STANLEY!
PWOARH!
HIGH FIVE!
RF

JANUARY/FEBRUARY • WEEK 5

monday 29	
tuesday 30	
wednesday 31	○
thursday 1	
friday 2	
saturday 3	
sunday 4	

JANUARY

M	T	W	T	F	S	S
1	2	3	4	5	6	7
8	9	10	11	12	13	14
15	16	17	18	19	20	21
22	23	24	25	26	27	28
29	30	31				

FEBRUARY • WEEK 6

monday 5	
tuesday 6	Accession of Queen Elizabeth II Holiday, New Zealand (Waitangi Day)
wednesday 7	☾
thursday 8	
friday 9	
saturday 10	
sunday 11	

HERE COMES MY FAVOURITE BIT...
3....
2...
1...
CLUNK!
BLAST OFF
RF

FEBRUARY • WEEK 7

monday 12	
tuesday 13	Shrove Tuesday
wednesday 14	Valentine's Day Ash Wednesday
thursday 15	●
friday 16	Chinese New Year
saturday 17	
sunday 18	

FEBRUARY

M	T	W	T	F	S	S
			1	2	3	4
5	6	7	8	9	10	11
12	13	14	15	16	17	18
19	20	21	22	23	24	25
26	27	28				

FEBRUARY • WEEK 8

monday 19	Holiday, USA (Presidents' Day)
tuesday 20	
wednesday 21	
thursday 22	
friday 23	☽
saturday 24	
sunday 25	

THE NEXT CATEGORY IS...'ACTING ALL BIG AND TOUGH AND SCARY WHEN A CAT APPEARS' ...AND THE NOMINEES ARE...WEST HIGHLAND TERRIERS...YORKSHIRE TERRIERS...POODLES... AND DACHSHUNDS...
THE DOGSCARS AWARDS
RF

monday 26	
tuesday 27	
wednesday 28	
thursday 1	St David's Day
friday 2	○
saturday 3	
sunday 4	

FEBRUARY

M	T	W	T	F	S	S
			1	2	3	4
5	6	7	8	9	10	11
12	13	14	15	16	17	18
19	20	21	22	23	24	25
26	27	28				

monday 5	
tuesday 6	
wednesday 7	
thursday 8	
friday 9	☾
saturday 10	
sunday 11	Mothering Sunday, UK and Republic of Ireland

ALL RIGHT, YOU CAN START GETTING THE BAG READY NOW
THAT'S IT. PICK IT UP WHILE IT'S STILL NICE AND WARM
TIE ONE OF YOUR PRETTY LITTLE BOWS IN IT. GOOD GIRL
MY OWN PERSONAL POO SLAVE
RF

monday 12	Commonwealth Day
tuesday 13	
wednesday 14	
thursday 15	
friday 16	
saturday 17	St Patrick's Day ●
sunday 18	

MARCH

M	T	W	T	F	S	S
			1	2	3	4
5	6	7	8	9	10	11
12	13	14	15	16	17	18
19	20	21	22	23	24	25
26	27	28	29	30	31	

monday 19	Holiday, Northern Ireland and Republic of Ireland (St Patrick's Day)
tuesday 20	Vernal Equinox (Spring begins)
wednesday 21	
thursday 22	
friday 23	
saturday 24	☽
sunday 25	Palm Sunday British Summer Time begins

AT PUPPY SCHOOL...
TODAY'S LESSON
CHAOS AND DESTRUCTION
SO, MR LEIBOWITZ, WHAT YOU'RE SAYING IS THAT WHATEVER OUR OWNERS TELL US TO DO, WE SHOULD DO THE OPPOSITE, AND WE'LL NEVER GET IN SERIOUS TROUBLE BECAUSE WE ARE SO DAMN CUTE
PRECISELY
RF

monday
26

tuesday
27

wednesday
28

thursday
29

Maundy Thursday

friday
30

Good Friday
Holiday, UK, Canada, Australia and New Zealand

saturday
31

Holiday, Australia (Easter Saturday)
First day of Passover (Pesach) ○

sunday
1

Easter Sunday

MARCH

M	T	W	T	F	S	S
			1	2	3	4
5	6	7	8	9	10	11
12	13	14	15	16	17	18
19	20	21	22	23	24	25
26	27	28	29	30	31	

monday 2	Easter Monday Holiday, UK (exc. Scotland), Republic of Ireland, Australia and New Zealand
tuesday 3	
wednesday 4	
thursday 5	
friday 6	
saturday 7	
sunday 8	☾

SHOOTING WAS NEVER THE SAME AGAIN AFTER THE FORMATION OF THE GUN DOGS UNION

APRIL • WEEK 15

monday 9	
tuesday 10	
wednesday 11	
thursday 12	
friday 13	
saturday 14	
sunday 15	

APRIL

M	T	W	T	F	S	S
						1
2	3	4	5	6	7	8
9	10	11	12	13	14	15
16	17	18	19	20	21	22
23	24	25	26	27	28	29
30						

monday 16	●
tuesday 17	
wednesday 18	
thursday 19	
friday 20	
saturday 21	Birthday of Queen Elizabeth II
sunday 22	☽

RECEIVE
PROCESS
SHRED, SHRED, SHRED,
RIP, RIP, RIP,
DELIVER
HE'D BE LOST WITHOUT ME
RF

APRIL • WEEK 17

monday
23

St George's Day

tuesday
24

wednesday
25

Holiday, Australia and
New Zealand (Anzac Day)

thursday
26

friday
27

saturday
28

sunday
29

APRIL

M	T	W	T	F	S	S
						1
2	3	4	5	6	7	8
9	10	11	12	13	14	15
16	17	18	19	20	21	22
23	24	25	26	27	28	29
30						

APRIL/MAY • WEEK 18

monday 30	○
tuesday 1	
wednesday 2	
thursday 3	
friday 4	
saturday 5	
sunday 6	

WALKIES, HUGO! COME ON, IT'S A BEAUTIFUL, SUNNY MAY DAY! WALKIES, WALKIES, WALKIES!! WEE-WEES, POO-POOS!
A LITTLE LESS PATRONISING BY ANY CHANCE, DAVID?
RF

monday 7	Early Spring Bank Holiday, UK Holiday, Republic of Ireland
tuesday 8	☾
wednesday 9	
thursday 10	Ascension Day
friday 11	
saturday 12	
sunday 13	Mother's Day, USA, Canada, Australia and New Zealand

MAY

M	T	W	T	F	S	S
	1	2	3	4	5	6
7	8	9	10	11	12	13
14	15	16	17	18	19	20
21	22	23	24	25	26	27
28	29	30	31			

monday 14	
tuesday 15	●
wednesday 16	First day of Ramadân (subject to sighting of the moon)
thursday 17	
friday 18	
saturday 19	
sunday 20	Whit Sunday Feast of Weeks (Shavuot)

TIME TO HAVE SOME FUN
RF

MAY • WEEK 21

monday 21	Holiday, Canada (Victoria Day)
tuesday 22	☽
wednesday 23	
thursday 24	
friday 25	
saturday 26	
sunday 27	Trinity Sunday

MAY

M	T	W	T	F	S	S
	1	2	3	4	5	6
7	8	9	10	11	12	13
14	15	16	17	18	19	20
21	22	23	24	25	26	27
28	29	30	31			

MAY/JUNE • WEEK 22

monday 28	Spring Bank Holiday, UK Holiday, USA (Memorial Day)
tuesday 29	○
wednesday 30	
thursday 31	Corpus Christi
friday 1	
saturday 2	Coronation Day
sunday 3	

AT PUPPY SCHOOL...
THIS WEEK
SOCIAL SKILLS
TODAY WE ARE GOING TO FOCUS ON 'LISTENING SKILLS'
RF

JUNE • WEEK 23

monday 4	Holiday, Republic of Ireland Holiday, New Zealand (The Queen's Birthday)
tuesday 5	
wednesday 6	☾
thursday 7	
friday 8	
saturday 9	The Queen's Official Birthday (subject to confirmation)
sunday 10	

JUNE

M	T	W	T	F	S	S
				1	2	3
4	5	6	7	8	9	10
11	12	13	14	15	16	17
18	19	20	21	22	23	24
25	26	27	28	29	30	

JUNE • WEEK 24

monday 11	Holiday, Australia (The Queen's Birthday)
tuesday 12	
wednesday 13	●
thursday 14	
friday 15	Eid al-Fitr (end of Ramadân) (subject to sighting of the moon)
saturday 16	
sunday 17	Father's Day, UK, Republic of Ireland, USA and Canada

COME ON SIEGFRIED, MUMMY AND DADDY ARE TAKING YOU FOR A WALK!
FOR HEAVEN'S SAKE, WILL YOU PLEASE STOP CALLING YOURSELVES 'MUMMY AND DADDY'! YOU ARE NOT MY PARENTS!
I'M A PEDIGREE!
RF

JUNE • WEEK 25

monday 18	
tuesday 19	
wednesday 20	☽
thursday 21	Summer Solstice (Summer begins)
friday 22	
saturday 23	
sunday 24	

JUNE

M	T	W	T	F	S	S
				1	2	3
4	5	6	7	8	9	10
11	12	13	14	15	16	17
18	19	20	21	22	23	24
25	26	27	28	29	30	

JUNE/JULY • WEEK 26

monday 25	
tuesday 26	
wednesday 27	
thursday 28	○
friday 29	
saturday 30	
sunday 1	Canada Day

YOU SPEND TOO MUCH TIME WITH YOUR HEAD OUT OF THAT CAR WINDOW, ROY
RF

JULY • WEEK 27

monday 2	Holiday, Canada (Canada Day)
tuesday 3	
wednesday 4	Holiday, USA (Independence Day)
thursday 5	
friday 6	☾
saturday 7	
sunday 8	

JULY

M	T	W	T	F	S	S
						1
2	3	4	5	6	7	8
9	10	11	12	13	14	15
16	17	18	19	20	21	22
23	24	25	26	27	28	29
30	31					

monday 9	
tuesday 10	
wednesday 11	
thursday 12	Holiday, Northern Ireland (Battle of the Boyne)
friday 13	●
saturday 14	
sunday 15	St Swithin's Day

INSIDE THE CANINE PRISON...
CAN YOU IMAGINE HOW HORRIBLE IT FEELS TO BE CHASED UP A TREE?
RF
AS PART OF THEIR REHABILITATION PROGRAM, INMATES WERE EXPECTED TO MEET THEIR VICTIMS

JULY • WEEK 29

monday 16	
tuesday 17	
wednesday 18	
thursday 19	☽
friday 20	
saturday 21	
sunday 22	

JULY

M	T	W	T	F	S	S
						1
2	3	4	5	6	7	8
9	10	11	12	13	14	15
16	17	18	19	20	21	22
23	24	25	26	27	28	29
30	31					

JULY • WEEK 30

monday 23	
tuesday 24	
wednesday 25	
thursday 26	
friday 27	○
saturday 28	
sunday 29	

I GUESS THIS IS WHAT THEY CALL 'BIKINI WEATHER'
DON'T DO IT, BORIS – YOU'LL LOOK RIDICULOUS
RF

JULY/AUGUST • WEEK 31

monday 30	
tuesday 31	
wednesday 1	
thursday 2	
friday 3	
saturday 4	☾
sunday 5	

JULY

M	T	W	T	F	S	S
						1
2	3	4	5	6	7	8
9	10	11	12	13	14	15
16	17	18	19	20	21	22
23	24	25	26	27	28	29
30	31					

monday 6	Holiday, Scotland and Republic of Ireland
tuesday 7	
wednesday 8	
thursday 9	
friday 10	
saturday 11	
sunday 12	

BRIAN, CAN YOU STOP LICKING MY FOOT. I'VE ALREADY TOLD YOU I'M NOT IN THE MOOD
RF

AUGUST • WEEK 33

monday 13	
tuesday 14	
wednesday 15	
thursday 16	
friday 17	
saturday 18	☽
sunday 19	

AUGUST

M	T	W	T	F	S	S
		1	2	3	4	5
6	7	8	9	10	11	12
13	14	15	16	17	18	19
20	21	22	23	24	25	26
27	28	29	30	31		

AUGUST • WEEK 34

monday 20	
tuesday 21	
wednesday 22	
thursday 23	
friday 24	
saturday 25	
sunday 26	○

NOW ALL I NEED IS A BIKE
RF

monday 27	Summer Bank Holiday, UK (exc. Scotland)
tuesday 28	
wednesday 29	
thursday 30	
friday 31	
saturday 1	
sunday 2	Father's Day, Australia and New Zealand

AUGUST

M	T	W	T	F	S	S
		1	2	3	4	5
6	7	8	9	10	11	12
13	14	15	16	17	18	19
20	21	22	23	24	25	26
27	28	29	30	31		

SEPTEMBER • WEEK 36

monday 3	Holiday, USA (Labor Day) Holiday, Canada (Labour Day) ☾
tuesday 4	
wednesday 5	
thursday 6	
friday 7	
saturday 8	
sunday 9	●

CUDDLE?
CUDDLE?
CUDDLE?
YOU KNOW YOU WANTED TO
RF

SEPTEMBER • WEEK 37

monday
10
Jewish New Year (Rosh Hashanah)

tuesday
11

wednesday
12
Islamic New Year

thursday
13

friday
14

saturday
15

sunday
16
☽

SEPTEMBER

M	T	W	T	F	S	S
					1	2
3	4	5	6	7	8	9
10	11	12	13	14	15	16
17	18	19	20	21	22	23
24	25	26	27	28	29	30

monday 17	
tuesday 18	
wednesday 19	Day of Atonement (Yom Kippur)
thursday 20	
friday 21	
saturday 22	
sunday 23	Autumnal Equinox (Autumn begins)

I NEED TO GET
IN TOUCH WITH
MY INNER PUPPY
RF

SEPTEMBER • WEEK 39

monday
24
First day of Tabernacles (Succoth)

tuesday
25
○

wednesday
26

thursday
27

friday
28

saturday
29
Michaelmas Day

sunday
30

SEPTEMBER

M	T	W	T	F	S	S
					1	2
3	4	5	6	7	8	9
10	11	12	13	14	15	16
17	18	19	20	21	22	23
24	25	26	27	28	29	30

OCTOBER • WEEK 40

monday 1	
tuesday 2	☾
wednesday 3	
thursday 4	
friday 5	
saturday 6	
sunday 7	

WHAT ARE YOU DOING THIS WEEK, PHIL?
ABSOLUTELY NOTHING!
ME TOO. I GUESS I'D BETTER GET STARTED
YEP, WE DON'T WANT TO GET BEHIND
RF

OCTOBER • WEEK 41

monday 8	Holiday, USA (Columbus Day) Holiday, Canada (Thanksgiving)
tuesday 9	●
wednesday 10	
thursday 11	
friday 12	
saturday 13	
sunday 14	

OCTOBER

M	T	W	T	F	S	S
1	2	3	4	5	6	7
8	9	10	11	12	13	14
15	16	17	18	19	20	21
22	23	24	25	26	27	28
29	30	31				

OCTOBER • WEEK 42

monday 15	
tuesday 16	☽
wednesday 17	
thursday 18	
friday 19	
saturday 20	
sunday 21	

SAUSAGE DOG NIGHTMARES

OCTOBER • WEEK 43

monday 22	Holiday, New Zealand (Labour Day)
tuesday 23	
wednesday 24	○
thursday 25	
friday 26	
saturday 27	
sunday 28	British Summer Time ends

OCTOBER

M	T	W	T	F	S	S
1	2	3	4	5	6	7
8	9	10	11	12	13	14
15	16	17	18	19	20	21
22	23	24	25	26	27	28
29	30	31				

OCTOBER/NOVEMBER • WEEK 44

monday 29	Holiday, Republic of Ireland
tuesday 30	
wednesday 31	Halloween ☾
thursday 1	All Saints' Day
friday 2	
saturday 3	
sunday 4	

PRE-ELECTION DEBATE
MY PRIORITIES ARE A STRONG ECONOMY, A ROBUST DEFENCE CAPABILITY, SENSIBLE FOREIGN POLICY, FREE HEALTHCARE FOR THE POOR AND ZERO UNEMPLOYMENT
I WANT US ALL TO LIE BACK ON THE FLOOR AND HAVE OUR BELLIES SCRATCHED THREE TIMES A DAY!
I'M LIKING THE GUY ON THE RIGHT
ME TOO
RF

NOVEMBER • WEEK 45

monday 5	Guy Fawkes
tuesday 6	
wednesday 7	●
thursday 8	
friday 9	
saturday 10	
sunday 11	Remembrance Sunday

NOVEMBER

M	T	W	T	F	S	S
			1	2	3	4
5	6	7	8	9	10	11
12	13	14	15	16	17	18
19	20	21	22	23	24	25
26	27	28	29	30		

NOVEMBER • WEEK 46

monday 12	Holiday, USA (Veterans Day) Holiday, Canada (Remembrance Day)
tuesday 13	
wednesday 14	
thursday 15	☽
friday 16	
saturday 17	
sunday 18	

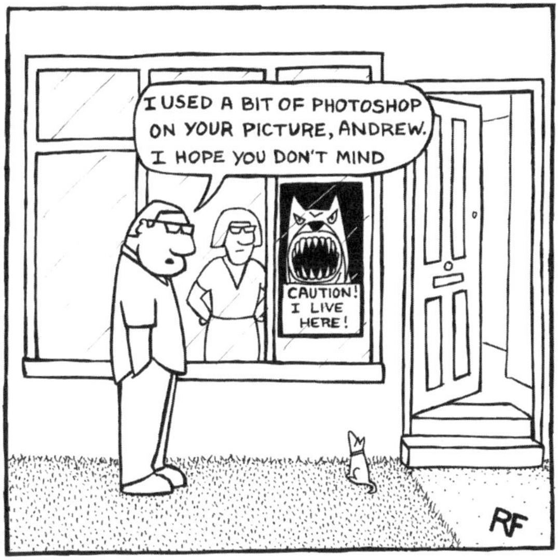
I USED A BIT OF PHOTOSHOP ON YOUR PICTURE, ANDREW. I HOPE YOU DON'T MIND
CAUTION! I LIVE HERE!
RF

NOVEMBER • WEEK 47

monday
19

tuesday
20

wednesday
21

thursday
22

Holiday, USA (Thanksgiving)

friday
23

○

saturday
24

sunday
25

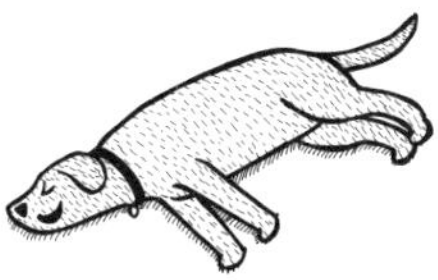

NOVEMBER

M	T	W	T	F	S	S
			1	2	3	4
5	6	7	8	9	10	11
12	13	14	15	16	17	18
19	20	21	22	23	24	25
26	27	28	29	30		

monday 26	
tuesday 27	
wednesday 28	
thursday 29	
friday 30	St Andrew's Day ☾
saturday 1	
sunday 2	First Sunday in Advent Hannukah begins (at sunset)

HEY, GUYS, I APPRECIATE YOU TELLING ME ABOUT YOUR EATING DISORDERS SUPPORT GROUP, BUT I REALLY DON'T HAVE A PROBLEM. I'M A GREYHOUND!
DENIAL
RF

DECEMBER • WEEK 49

monday 3	
tuesday 4	
wednesday 5	
thursday 6	
friday 7	
saturday 8	
sunday 9	

DECEMBER

M	T	W	T	F	S	S
					1	2
3	4	5	6	7	8	9
10	11	12	13	14	15	16
17	18	19	20	21	22	23
24	25	26	27	28	29	30
31						

DECEMBER • WEEK 50

monday 10	Hannukah ends
tuesday 11	
wednesday 12	
thursday 13	
friday 14	
saturday 15	☽
sunday 16	

COME ON, PLUTO. LET'S GET OUT THERE!
THE SNOW'S TOO DEEP
LET'S BE BRAVE BOY!
THE SNOW'S TOO DEEP
GO BACK! THE SNOW'S TOO DEEP!
AND THESE PEOPLE RUN THE PLANET
RF

DECEMBER • WEEK 51

monday
17

tuesday
18

wednesday
19

thursday
20

friday
21

Winter Solstice (Winter begins)

saturday
22

○

sunday
23

DECEMBER

M	T	W	T	F	S	S
					1	2
3	4	5	6	7	8	9
10	11	12	13	14	15	16
17	18	19	20	21	22	23
24	25	26	27	28	29	30
31						

monday 24	Christmas Eve
tuesday 25	Christmas Day Holiday, UK, Republic of Ireland, USA, Canada, Australia and New Zealand
wednesday 26	Boxing Day (St Stephen's Day) Holiday, UK, Republic of Ireland, Canada, Australia and New Zealand
thursday 27	
friday 28	
saturday 29	☾
sunday 30	

THE THREE WISE DOGS...
OH, COLIN! FOR HEAVEN'S SAKE! CAN'T THAT WAIT?
RF

monday
31

New Year's Eve

tuesday
1

New Year's Day
Holiday, UK, Republic of Ireland, USA, Canada, Australia and New Zealand

wednesday
2

Holiday, Scotland and New Zealand

thursday
3

friday
4

saturday
5

sunday
6

Epiphany ●

JANUARY 2019

M	T	W	T	F	S	S
	1	2	3	4	5	6
7	8	9	10	11	12	13
14	15	16	17	18	19	20
21	22	23	24	25	26	27
28	29	30	31			

I WANT SOME ATTENTION!
I SAID, 'I WANT SOME ATTENTION'!
STOP IGNORING ME!
RF

DON'T BE RIDICULOUS BERTIE, THAT'S MUCH TOO BIG FOR YOU!
NEVER UNDERESTIMATE THE POWER, STRENGTH AND DETERMINATION OF A JACK RUSSELL, MY FRIEND
RF

MEEAOWW!